AF270600

NEW ENGLAND
PATRIOTS
PATRIOTS
37
KENNY ABDO
Fly!
An Imprint of Abdo Zoom
abdobooks.com

# abdobooks.com

Published by Abdo Zoom, a division of ABDO, P.O. Box 398166, Minneapolis, Minnesota 55439. Copyright © 2022 by Abdo Consulting Group, Inc. International copyrights reserved in all countries. No part of this book may be reproduced in any form without written permission from the publisher. Fly!™ is a trademark and logo of Abdo Zoom.

Printed in the United States of America, North Mankato, Minnesota.
052021
092021

Photo Credits: Getty Images, Icon Sportswire, iStock, Shutterstock PREMIER
Production Contributors: Kenny Abdo, Jennie Forsberg, Grace Hansen
Design Contributors: Candice Keimig, Neil Klinepier

**Library of Congress Control Number: 2020919501**

**Publisher's Cataloging-in-Publication Data**

Names: Abdo, Kenny, author.
Title: New England Patriots / by Kenny Abdo
Description: Minneapolis, Minnesota : Abdo Zoom, 2022 | Series: NFL teams | Includes online resources and index.
Identifiers: ISBN 9781098224721 (lib. bdg.) | ISBN 9781098225667 (ebook) | ISBN 9781098226138 (Read-to-Me ebook)
Subjects: LCSH: New England Patriots (Football team)--Juvenile literature. | National Football League--Juvenile literature. | Football teams--Juvenile literature. | American football--Juvenile literature. | Professional sports--Juvenile literature.
Classification: DDC 796.33264--dc23

# TABLE OF CONTENTS

# NEW ENGLAND PATRIOTS

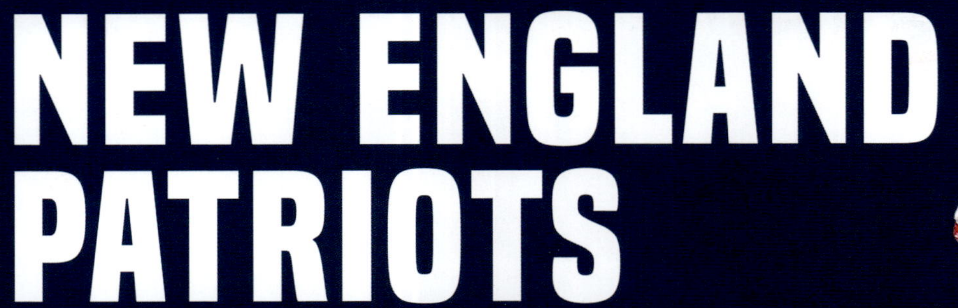

Considered a powerhouse of the NFL, the New England Patriots have the records and wins to back it up.

Representing the six northeastern states of New England, the Patriots have built a football dynasty of historic size!

# KICK OFF

Boston was awarded a football team by the American Football League (AFL) in 1959. The public named them the Boston Patriots. The team played the San Diego Chargers in the 1963 AFL **Championship**, but lost 51–10.

In 1971, the team moved to the nearby city of Foxborough. The Boston Patriots changed its name to the New England Patriots to include the entire region.

The Patriots found some success in their new home. The team went to the **divisional** playoffs in the 1976 season. They lost to the Raiders 24-21.

# TEAM RECAPS

The Patriots grew stronger as a team. Through many highs and lows, they would become the only team to make it to the **Super Bowl** a record 11 times!

The Patriots won their first **Super Bowl** following the 2001 season! They beat the St. Louis Rams 20-17 with a last second field goal.

The Patriots went to back-to-back **Super Bowls** after the 2003 and 2004 seasons. They won both games by just three points!

TRABEL
50

LII
SUPER BOWL
BOWL
CHAMPIONS
WE ARE ALL PATRIOTS

The Patriots made yet another **Super Bowl** appearance, beating the Seahawks at Super Bowl XLIX. Coming back from a 25 point deficit, they beat the Falcons 34-28 in Super Bowl LI. Tom Brady collected his fourth Big Game **MVP**!

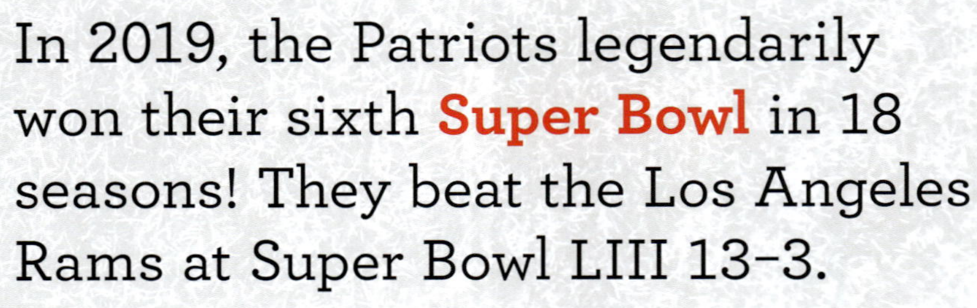

In 2019, the Patriots legendarily won their sixth **Super Bowl** in 18 seasons! They beat the Los Angeles Rams at Super Bowl LIII 13–3.

The 2020 season was the first time the team played without Tom Brady since 2001. They ended the season with a 7-9 record, breaking an 11-year streak of playoff appearances.

# HALL OF FAME

Andre Tippett played for the Patriots his entire career. Tippett had 100 **sacks** in his 11 seasons. That is more than any other Patriot! He also went to five Pro Bowls during his career. Tippett was **inducted** into the Pro Football Hall of Fame in 2008.

NFL
NFL
ALUMNI
PRO FOOTBALL
HALL OF FAME
ENSHRINEE
PRO FOOTBALL
HALL OF FAME
CANTON OHIO

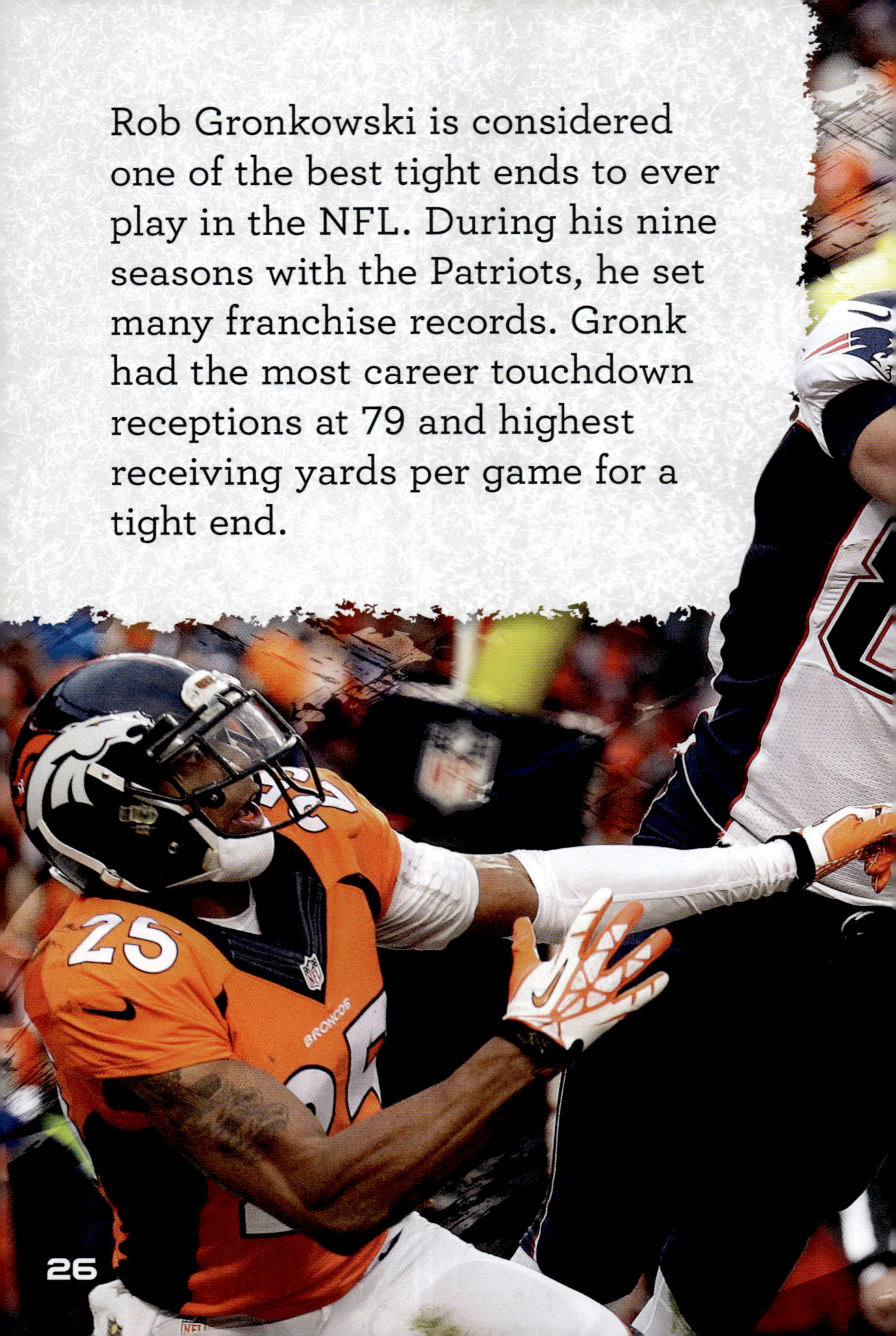

Rob Gronkowski is considered one of the best tight ends to ever play in the NFL. During his nine seasons with the Patriots, he set many franchise records. Gronk had the most career touchdown receptions at 79 and highest receiving yards per game for a tight end.

Tom Brady became the Patriots' starting **quarterback** in 2001. In 2005, Sports Illustrated named him Sportsman of the Year. Brady led the team to six **Super Bowl** victories. Brady is the NFL's all-time leader in playoff wins (30), touchdown passes (73), and passing yards (11,179) with the Patriots.

# GLOSSARY

**championship** – a game held to find a first-place winner.

**division** – a group of teams who compete against each other for a championship.

**induct** – to admit someone as a member of an organization.

**MVP** – short for "most valuable player," an award given in sports to a player who has performed the best in a game or series.

**quarterback (QB)** – the player on the offensive team that directs teammates in their play.

**sack** – when a quarterback is tackled behind the line of scrimmage while still in possession of the ball.

**Super Bowl** – the NFL championship game, played once a year.

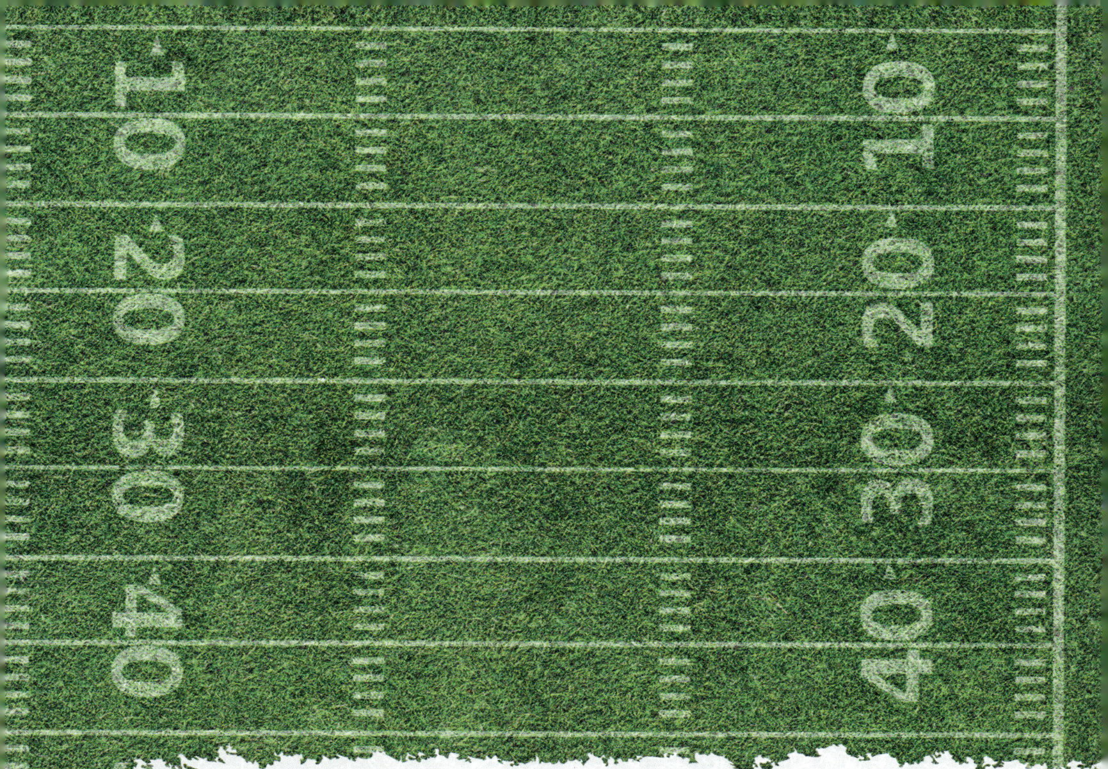

# ONLINE RESOURCES

To learn more about the New England Patriots, please visit **abdobooklinks. com** or scan this QR code. These links are routinely monitored and updated to provide the most current information available.

# INDEX